BRAIN GAME TREASURE HUNTS

SPACE PUZZLES

Senior Editor: Alice Peebles
Designer: www.collaborate.agency

Text and Puzzle copyright © 2016 Dr. Gareth Moore
Original edition copyright 2016 by Hungry Tomato Ltd.

Hungry Tomato™
A division of Lerner Publishing Group, Inc.
241 First Avenue North
Minneapolis, MN 55401 USA

For reading levels and more information, look up
this title at www.lernerbooks.com.

Main body text set in Eurostile Regular 11/11.5.
Typeface provided by Microsoft.

Library of Congress Cataloging-in-Publication Data
Names: Moore, Gareth, 1975- author.
Title: Space puzzles / by Dr. Gareth Moore.
Description: Minneapolis : Hungry Tomato, [2017] | Series: Brain game treasure
   hunts | Audience: Ages 8-12. | Audience: Grades 4 to 6. | Includes index.
Identifiers: LCCN 2015046266 (print) | LCCN 2015048648 (ebook) | ISBN
   9781512406245 (lb : alk. paper) | ISBN 9781512411744 (pb : alk. paper) |
   ISBN 9781512409307 (eb pdf)
Subjects: LCSH: Astronautics--Juvenile literature. | Logic puzzles--Juvenile
   literature. | Puzzles--Juvenile literature.
Classification: LCC TL793 .M6274 2017 (print) | LCC TL793 (ebook) | DDC
   629.4/102--dc23
LC record available at http://lccn.loc.gov/2015046266

Manufactured in United States of America
1-39297-21134-5/3/2016

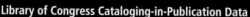

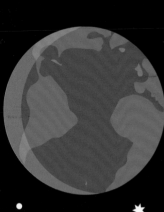

BRAIN GAME TREASURE HUNTS

SPACE PUZZLES

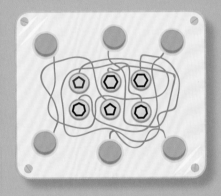

by Dr. Gareth Moore

HUNGRY TOMATO™

Minneapolis

CONTENTS

SPACE PUZZLES INTRODUCTION

"Welcome to NASA!" announces the sign as you enter the space exploration center. You've been invited on a unique behind-the-scenes tour. You'll even get to put on a real space suit and sit on the control deck of the latest experimental spaceship!

This is a special kind of book. It contains a story with lots of puzzles, but these aren't normal puzzles like you will have seen before. These puzzles don't tell you exactly what to do—they provide only a certain amount of information, and then it's up to you to work out what to do and how to solve them!

If you get stuck or aren't sure how to solve a puzzle, there are hints provided. The hints are an important part of each puzzle, and you will need them for at least a few of the puzzles. When reading the hints for a puzzle, read them one at a time and only read the later hints if you are still stuck. Working out what to do is part of the fun!

MILESTONES IN SPACE

1957 – First animal in orbit

1959 – First lunar probe

1961 – First person in space

1966 – First lunar soft landing

1969 – First person on the moon

PST **EST** **GMT** **CET**

WORLD CLOCKS:

PST – Pacific Standard Time (-8:00)

EST – Eastern Standard Time (-5:00)

GMT – Greenwich Mean Time (+0:00)

CET – Central European Time (+1:00)

PREPARING FOR LAUNCH

Your tour has taken you to the cockpit of the latest developmental Planet X spaceship. You can't resist pressing a few buttons to see what it feels like to be an astronaut—and you're already wearing the latest NASA space suit.

Suddenly the floor starts shuddering, and an alarm sounds. A voice reaches you inside the space suit's helmet: *"Launch sequence started—open bay doors for takeoff."*

It looks like you've accidentally put the spaceship into launch mode! Quick, you must open the bay doors so the ship can exit the building without destroying the entire facility! Rotate the dials to match the door-opening sequence on the panel below.

You need to open the bay doors. The control dials look like this:

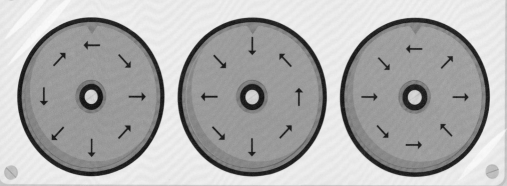

Next to the dials is a panel of options:

↖ ↓ ↙	↗ ← ↓	↑ → ←
↓ → ↓	↓ → ←	→ ← ↓
↗ ↗ ↓	↖ ↓ →	← ↓ ↗
↖ ↙ ↑	↑ ← →	↓ ↖ ↖
↓ → ↑	↓ ← ↓	↖ → ←
→ ↓ →	↖ ↑ ←	→ ← →

Only one of the options on the panel to the left is correct. Can you work out which one?

Remember that you need to rotate the dials. The arrows will rotate too!

You open the doors, but almost immediately a warning appears on the control panel:

DOCKING CLAMPS OVERRIDE REQUIRED

You pick up the pilot's manual and quickly find *"Docking clamps—override"* in the index.

The manual tells you to release the clamps in the order 1, 2, 3, and features the following wiring diagram, showing how the clamps are connected:

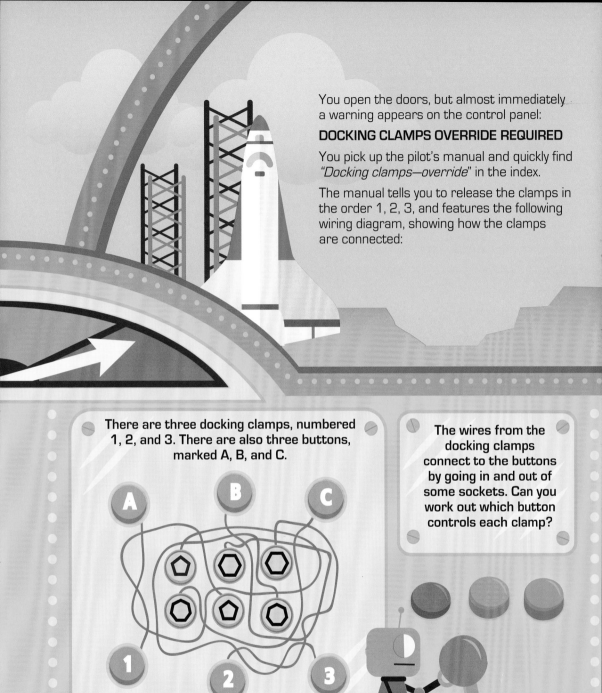

There are three docking clamps, numbered 1, 2, and 3. There are also three buttons, marked A, B, and C.

The wires from the docking clamps connect to the buttons by going in and out of some sockets. Can you work out which button controls each clamp?

After solving the wiring diagram puzzle, you press the buttons in the correct order and unlock the docking clamps. Now your ship can safely leave the launch tower without taking the tower along too!

LAUNCH ▶▶▶

NEED THE SOLUTION? Turn to page 30.

BLAST OFF

The spaceship's computer needs to know your exact launch coordinates.

By using the map to the right and the information below, can you work out your launch coordinates?

LAUNCH COORDINATES

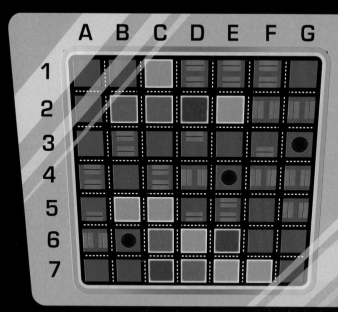

You remember the final part of your journey to the launch site:

1. Starting from the point where your route came into view on the map above, you traveled between two gray office buildings and then turned right.

2. You drove one block and then turned left.

3. You kept driving until you passed a blue lake on your left. Then you immediately turned left.

4. You drove at least two blocks, then turned right immediately after passing an empty green, grassy block on your right.

5. You then drove until you passed a gray office building on your right, at which point you immediately turned right

6. You drove two and a half blocks, then parked and entered the office building on your right. It was this building that contained the NASA launch facility.

Using the above, can you work out where you launched from? Use the coordinates outside the window to write down the correct grid location to enter into the navigation computer.

Now the ship's computer wants to know your chosen destination. To do this, you must choose one of six potential destination codes:

DESTINATION CODE

In the pilot's manual you find a list of destination codes, each consisting of three letters. You think it would be fun to go the moon, which has the code CEG. Unfortunately, something is wrong with the computer, and it isn't displaying the codes correctly.

Each of the six codes above consists of three letters, but the letters have all been changed in some way to disguise them. The computer is informing you that it has a "reflection display error." Does that help you identify which is CEG?

You pick a code, and it is correct! The computer confirms:
YOU'RE GOING TO THE MOON!

DESTINATION: MOON

The computer sets a flight path for the moon. As you leave Earth's atmosphere, you admire the incredible view of the curve of the planet's surface and realize just how much of the Earth is covered by ocean.

Suddenly an alarm sounds, and a warning appears, saying that manual navigation assistance is required. You will need to navigate using the stars!

In the pilot's manual you find a star chart that shows eight constellations:

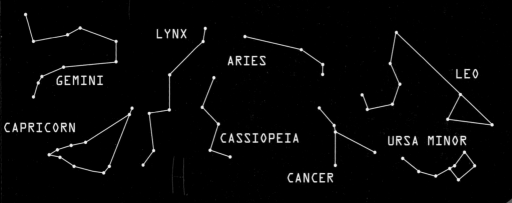

LYNX
ARIES
GEMINI
LEO
CAPRICORN
CASSIOPEIA
URSA MINOR
CANCER

ODD STAR CHART

- 4
- 23
- 2
- 22
- 10
- 18
- 26
- 11
- 8
- 19
- 34
- 3
- 14
- 38
- 7

The computer has produced a printout that you can use to work out which of these constellations you should use as your navigation reference.

Unfortunately the information has been encoded, and you will need to decode it first.

Can you make sense of this "odd" star chart? Have you ever seen numbered dots before? Which star constellation should you be heading toward?

You choose the correct star constellation, but the navigation computer now requires some numerical information to finalize your exact course.

It needs five numbers in order to point the ship's rockets in the correct direction.

The computer produces a second printout that shows the series of calculations required to find each of the five values. Start at the number on the left of each row, then apply each operation in turn:

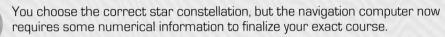

ROCKET SCIENCE

Work out the five values that the navigation computer needs in order to continue the trip to the moon.

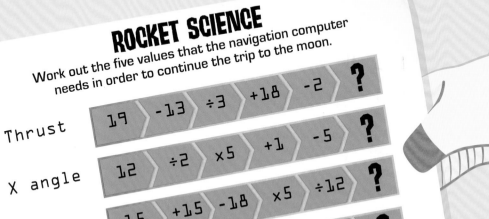

Thrust   19 ⟩ -13 ⟩ ÷3 ⟩ +18 ⟩ -2 ⟩ **?**

X angle   12 ⟩ ÷2 ⟩ ×5 ⟩ +1 ⟩ -5 ⟩ **?**

Y angle   15 ⟩ +15 ⟩ -18 ⟩ ×5 ⟩ ÷12 ⟩ **?**

Z angle   19 ⟩ -7 ⟩ ÷3 ⟩ +5 ⟩ -3 ⟩ **?**

Burn time   5 ⟩ ×12 ⟩ ÷6 ⟩ +7 ⟩ ×2 ⟩ **?**

You complete your calculations in your head, since you don't have a pen or paper handy, and enter them into the navigation computer.

The computer ignites the rocket boosters and adjusts the course of the spaceship.

Before long the moon starts to fill the view from the spaceship's windows. You're nearly there!

LUNAR LANDING

Your spaceship enters orbit around the moon, but before it can land, a warning appears on the computer screen:

LANDING FUEL BLOCKAGE!
-> SUPPLY 6 GALLONS

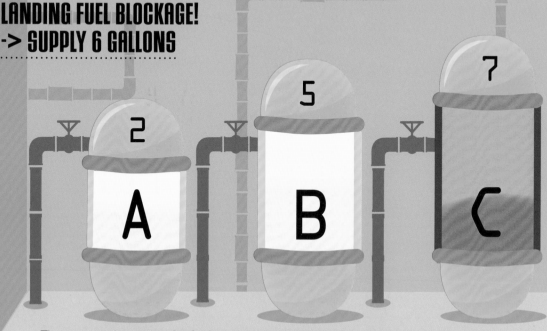

The screen shows you the fuel management system that can move fuel between three containers, labeled A, B, and C. The containers can store 2, 5, and 7 gallons, as shown above. Container A can hold 2 gallons, container B can hold 5 gallons, and container C can hold 7 gallons.

MEASURING FUEL

Container C is filled with 7 gallons of fuel, but containers A and B are empty. To help the ship land, you need to work out how to measure out exactly 6 gallons of fuel.

The motorized system will transfer from one container to another until **either** the destination container is full **or** the source container is empty.

This means that if you were to start by transferring from container C to container A, you would end up with 2 gallons in container A and 5 gallons in container C. You can't stop the transfer part way.

Can you work out how to measure exactly 6 gallons of fuel into one of the containers? You can do this in just five moves, but what is this five-move solution?

With the correct amount of fuel in the largest container, you tell the computer to proceed. But the computer now needs to balance the fuel supply to each of the six landing thrusters in order to keep the spaceship level for a stable landing.

BALANCING FUEL LEVELS

The computer has some partial information about how the engine fuel levels should be balanced, which it presents to you in the form of four seesaw balance diagrams:

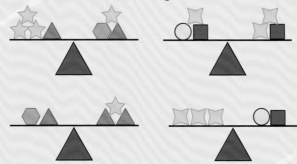

It also knows the correct values for two of the thrusters, so it tells you that the red triangle has a weight of 2 pounds, and the four-pointed star has a weight of 3 pounds.

Given the weight information from the seesaw balances, can you work out how much each of the four other shapes weighs?

Once you've worked out the correct values, the ship is ready to land on the moon! It proceeds to head down towards the lunar surface, landing with a gentle bump.

ON THE MOON

While you're on the moon, you'll need to refuel the ship so that you can return to Earth.

The ship informs you that there is a NASA supply base nearby. You'll need to leave the ship and travel across the surface of the moon to get some fuel pods.

DOOR LOCK MECHANISM

To open the exit hatch, you must find the combination of button presses that will result in all of the items on each panel having the same value. The four panels looks like this:

There are eight buttons, two per panel, and four handwritten notes added in gray pen—these are probably important!

Next to the panel is a series of possible button presses:

You look at the handwritten notes and feel sure that these must be a clue. Written in bold letters on the wall next to the panel are two words: **TIME** and **TRAVEL**. Perhaps these numbers are times? But what does traveling have to do with it?

```
- - / - - - - - / + + / + +
  + + / - / - / - - / - -
- - - / - - - - / - - - / - -
  + + + + / - / + / + +
  + + + / - - / + / -
+ / - - - - - / - - - / - - -
```

Do you understand how the panel operates? Can you work out what the handwritten messages mean? And can you understand how to read the button press options? There are six options, one per row. Which one will open the exit hatch?

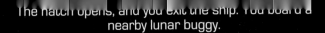

The hatch opens, and you exit the ship. You board a nearby lunar buggy.

The buggy is specially adapted to the lunar surface and can only drive in straight lines. It will drive continuously until it reaches an obstacle. At this point you can turn it 90 degrees left or right and then continue.

The lunar plain is laid out as in the grid below. The buggy enters from the left, as shown by the arrows, and must exit from the right. The quickest route would be to drive straight across in the fifth row down, but there is a problem...

LUNAR PLAIN

The buggy runs on experimental fuel and must use up most of it before crossing the plain. This means it can't take the route straight across the center. Instead it needs to find the **longest** route across from left to right. This route will involve stopping at obstacles eighteen times.

You can enter the plain at any of the arrows on the left and exit at any of the arrows on the right.

You can't stop the buggy in the same square more than once.

You find the safe route and arrive at a supply hangar.

SEARCHING FOR FUEL

When you reach the hangar, you find a door that is locked. There is a security panel beside it that seems to provide a way to gain entry.

The panel looks like this:

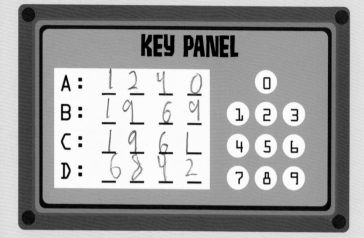

KEY PANEL

A : 1 2 4 0
B : 1 9 6 9
C : 1 9 6 4
D : 6 8 4 2

0
1 2 3
4 5 6
7 8 9

You're not quite sure what to enter, but when you look around, you see an ID card lying on the ground beneath the panel. There's no wind or rain on the moon, so this could have been here for a long time!

On the back of the card, someone has scribbled down some clues to remind them of the security panel access codes:

The 1st human in space—that's Charlie!

Won too for nothing at Alpha!

Bravo—first man on the Moon!

Delta was sicks! Ate for two!

What should you enter to unlock the door?

These clues correspond in some way to the digits you need to enter to unlock the door. Can you work out exactly what you should type in to open the door?

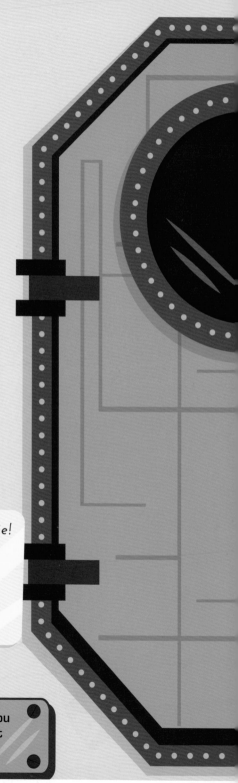

You key in the correct security codes, and the door makes a grinding sound before slowly opening. You step through into a small entrance room, which brings you face-to-face with a second door. As the door behind you starts to close, the panel on the second door lights up as follows:

SECURITY PANEL

1	8	3	7	9	6
3	4	8	0	1	4
7	8	3	2	6	5
4	2	7	9	0	3
_	_	_	_	_	_

0
1 2 3
4 5 6
7 8 9

This security lock must use a different system from the previous one, so what is the correct code? You turn to the ID card you found before, and this time you pay more attention to some crossed-out numbers on the front. They look like this:

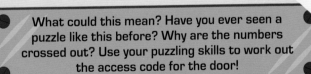

~~4887~~ ~~612~~ ~~3097~~

~~1837~~ 743 ~~94~~

What could this mean? Have you ever seen a puzzle like this before? Why are the numbers crossed out? Use your puzzling skills to work out the access code for the door!

You finally work out the correct code for the panel. You key it in and are rewarded by the sight of the second door sliding open to reveal the interior of the hangar.

INTO THE HANGAR ▶▶▶

THE MOON'S HANGAR

The hangar is extremely dark. The building is in HIBERNATE mode. You need to set up the lighting system.

To do this, you must enter a four-digit code into the lighting control panel. To obtain the code, you need to work out how to read the systems diagram displayed alongside it. It is already configured with an initial five-digit input code, but the four-digit output code is not shown:

LIGHTING SYSTEM

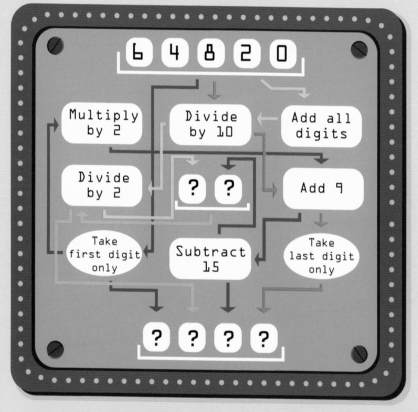

Can you work out how to read this diagram? What is the final four-digit code you need to use to switch on the lighting system?

With the correct code, the lights come on! But the computer has lost part of its programming and will need to be set up again. It knows the number of each room, but not its name.

A wall display shows the thirteen room names:

3 x Silo
2 x Laboratory
1 x Recreation Room
1 x Waste Disposal
1 x Cafe
1 x Medical Facility
1 x Safe Room
1 x Crew Supplies
1 x Tool Storage
1 x Guard Room

HANGAR MAP

The hangar contains thirteen rooms and a large amount of corridor space:

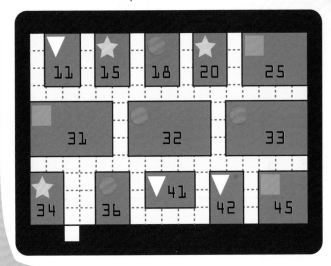

Can you work out which room is which on the map?
Some notes pinned to the wall tell you that:

1. The Guard Room touches two exterior walls.

2. The two Laboratories are both the same size, and there are no other rooms between them.

3. The Recreation Room is located directly between one of the Silos and the Waste Disposal.

4. The room number of the Crew Supplies room is lower than that of the Cafe.

5. If you add the room number of one of the Laboratories to the room number of the Medical Facility, the result is the same as the sum of the room numbers of the Recreation Room and Tool Storage.

6. The Safe Room is marked with a circle.

7. The number of the Tool Storage room is greater than the sum of the room numbers of all three Silos.

8. The Waste Disposal room is exactly twice the size of the Cafe.

Assign one of the thirteen listed rooms to each of the numbered rooms on the map. All of the information you need is contained within the notes on the wall.

Success! All the doors in the hangar are now open, and you discover that the fuel is in Silo 1.

AUTOMATED CARTS

Inside the hangar, there are automated carts that pick you up and move you around on a grid-based system.

The cart requires a name and employee identity number in order to activate. You can use the name and number on your space suit, but you can't read it while wearing it.

However, you can see its reflection in the cart screen.

IDENTITY CODE

What is the identity number and name of the person whose space suit you are wearing?

Enter name and employee identity number to proceed

After you enter the details, the cart starts up. It displays a list of possible commands, which you can see on the opposite page.

The cart also displays a map of the complex that shows all the doors as well as the location of the fuel that you require. The map confirms your own location.

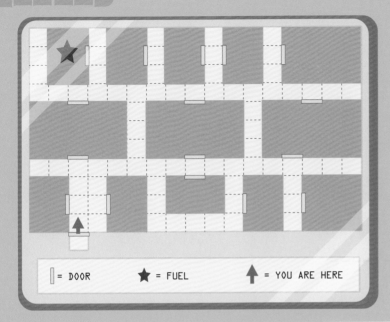

RETRIEVING THE FUEL

The hangar floor consists of a number of grid tile squares. You are currently in the marked square at bottom left, facing as per the arrow. You can only make the cart move by choosing one of five commands, A to E. Your job is to find a series of commands that will lead the cart to the room with the fuel.

AUTOMATED CART COMMANDS

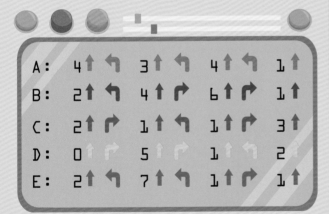

A: 4⬆ ↰ 3⬆ ↰ 4⬆ ↰ 1⬆

B: 2⬆ ↰ 4⬆ ↱ 6⬆ ↱ 1⬆

C: 2⬆ ↱ 1⬆ ↰ 1⬆ ↱ 3⬆

D: 0⬆ ↱ 5⬆ ↱ 1⬆ ↰ 2⬆

E: 2⬆ ↰ 7⬆ ↰ 1⬆ ↱ 1⬆

Each command consists of a series of moves. There are two types of move. Either the cart moves forward in the current direction for a given number of grid tile squares, or the cart turns 90 degrees on the spot to face in a new direction. For example, if you were to move 1 grid square forward, turn to the left, then move 1 grid square forward, you would end up in the room at the bottom left.

Use the command list to find a route to the fuel. You must avoid crashing the cart, so commands can't drive you into walls!

You program the cart with the correct route information, and it sets off to the destination room.

NEED THE SOLUTION? Turn to page 31.

LOADING THE FUEL

You are in the fuel silo, where a series of computerized control systems are provided to help you transport the fuel safely to your ship.

A small routing diagram is displayed on a computer console, as shown:

ROUTING DIAGRAMS

You study the image and notice that there are exactly two of each number, and each numbered pair is linked by a single path. You also notice that only one path enters any grid square. This is to make sure that none of the delicate fuel components accidentally collide. They must all follow separate routes that don't overlap.

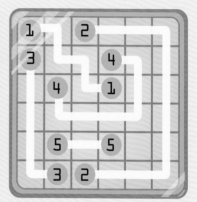

The screen suddenly resets and shows two new routing diagrams—except that both of these maps are missing the actual routes! They appear as follows:

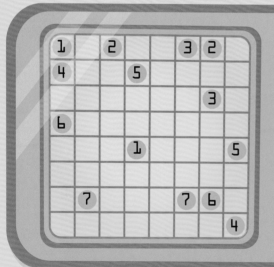

Copy each routing diagram onto a clean sheet of paper, drawing both the grid lines and the numbers and letters. Can you draw in all of the correct routing paths?

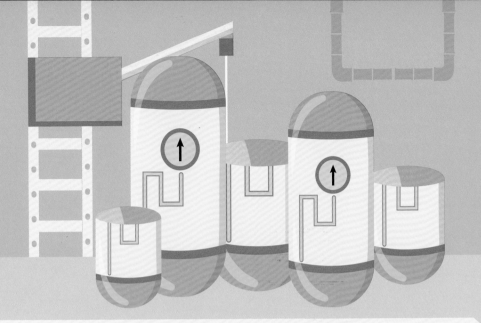

You complete the routing diagrams and enter the appropriate information into the computer.

A crane prepares to load fourteen fuel pods onto your cart, but it requires you to manually work out the best packing strategy.

LOADING PLAN

The fourteen fuel pods look like this:

The fuel pods are designed to fit together in pairs. Can you work out which pods fit together? In each pair, one of the two can be rotated 180 degrees to form a perfect fit on top of the other one.

Can you pair each fuel pod container up with the correct other half of its pair? Each fuel pod is labeled with a letter, so you can write down your solution as a series of pairs of letters.

Once the sequence of letter pairs is entered, the fuel pods are loaded, and the cart exits the hangar. It automatically finds its way back to the spaceship.

NEED THE SOLUTION? Turn to page 31.

RETURNING HOME

The fuel pods have been loaded successfully!

All you need to do now is program your journey back to Earth by entering a series of values into the computer (below). Then you'll need to do final calculations for THRUST and BURN TIME (below right).

You'll need to solve a puzzle to work out the correct values to program your homeward journey:

X ANGLE, Y ANGLE, and Z ANGLE

You need three numbers, one each for the X, Y, and Z angles of your launch vector. Each is a single digit from 1 to 5, and you must work out how to calculate them using this image from the pilot's flight manual:

PROGRAMMING YOUR JOURNEY HOME

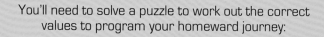

4	X	3	2	
5				
		3		
				4
2	5			3

		1		
	5	2	1	
1	4	5	3	2
	1	4	5	
		3		Y

	5		1	
3				5
Z		2		
1				4
	4		5	

The final calculations are complete and locked in, and you can now return to Earth. Your excellent problem-solving abilities have brought you home.

Welcome home, astronaut!

THRUST

To calculate the correct thrust, you need a five-digit number:

Digit 1 = the docking clamp connected to button B

Digit 2 = the final digit of D required to open the first hangar door

Digit 3 = a quarter of the total weight of the six different shapes in the fuel balance system

Digit 4 = half of the number of doors that open into hangar rooms

Digit 5 = a quarter of the number of red-roofed houses you could see on the map of your launch location

BURN TIME

To calculate the correct burn time, you need a second five-digit number:

Digit 1 = the first digit of the final dot connected to form a constellation

Digit 2 = the number of addition symbols in the code required to release the spaceship door lock

Digit 3 = half of the thrust you calculated on the way to the moon

Digit 4 = the sum of the last two digits used to enable the hangar lights

Digit 5 = the number of times you used command C when routing the cart to the fuel

You made it home—congratulations!

SPACE PUZZLES HINTS

Not sure how to solve a puzzle? Use these hints to help.

Each puzzle has a series of numbered hints. Read hint 1 first and see if it helps. Then only read each further hint if you still need it—each successive hint reveals more about how to solve the puzzle.

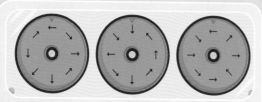

PAGES 6–7
BAY DOORS

1 The orange triangles above each dial show which arrow is currently selected by the dial.
2 When you turn the dials, the arrows that are drawn on them will rotate with the dial. The orange triangle will stay still and point at a different arrow.
3 Only one of the eighteen possible options on the panel can be created by turning the dials.
4 Can any orange triangle ever point at a diagonal arrow?
5 There are no diagonal arrows, so you can eliminate all the options with a diagonal arrow.
6 The left dial can't ever select a down arrow. The middle dial can't ever select a right-facing arrow. The right dial can't ever select a right-facing arrow.

PAGES 6–7
DOCKING CLAMPS

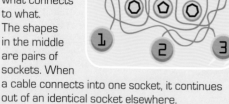

1 You need to follow the cable lines to see what connects to what.
2 The shapes in the middle are pairs of sockets. When a cable connects into one socket, it continues out of an identical socket elsewhere.

PAGES 8–9
LAUNCH COORDINATES

1 The hard part of this puzzle is working out where you started from.
2 You know you start traveling between two gray buildings, so the route must enter from the bottom of the map and head upward.
3 Start by traveling between the buildings in D7 and E7.
4 You then turn right, travel one block, turn left, and keep going until you pass a lake on the left, in E4.
5 Turn left and continue until you pass a grassy area on the right, which is C3.

PAGES 8–9
DESTINATION CODE

1 Do these symbols remind you of the letters around the map?
2 How can these letters be changed to look like the ones on the panel?
3 Imagine placing a mirror vertically over each letter.
4 Each letter has its left half reflected, hiding the right half.
5 So an A still looks the same, but the other letters have changed. The first symbol on the first row is a G, for example.

ODD STAR CHART

1 Why do you think it is labeled an "ODD STAR CHART"?
2 Odd is a clue to make you think of odd numbers.
3 What would you see if you were to join up all the odd numbers in numerical order?

ROCKET SCIENCE

19	-13	÷3	+18	-2	?
12	÷2	X5	+1	-5	?
15	+15	-18	X5	÷12	?
19	-7	÷3	+5	-3	?
5	X12	÷6	+7	X2	?

1 For Thrust, start with 19, subtract 13, divide by 3, add 18, and then subtract 2. Your answer is the result for Thrust.
Then do the same for each row.

MEASURING FUEL

1 The first move must be to move fuel from C to either A or B. Try moving it to B. This will leave 5 gallons in B and 2 gallons in C.
2 After moving from C to B, next move from B to A. Then add the 2 gallons from A to C, leaving 3 gallons in B and 4 gallons in C. You're nearly done!

BALANCING FUEL LEVELS

1 The top left balance shows that a hexagon weighs the same as two five-pointed stars.
2 Now you know the hexagon in the bottom left balance could be replaced with two stars, so you know that two stars and a triangle weigh the same as one star and two triangles. This means the five-pointed star and triangle have the same weight.

DOOR LOCK MECHANISM

1 The button presses show you how many times to press the + or – button on each panel. For example, - -/- - - - -/++/++ shows two presses on the PST panel, five on the GMT panel, two on the CET panel, and two on the EST panel.
2 Each + press advances a time by an hour. Each – press goes back an hour. So – – on the 12:00 dial gives 10:00.
3 These are 24-hour clocks, so pressing + on 23:00 will change to 00:00, and pressing – on 00:00 will change to 23:00.
4 If you try each of the six different sets of button presses, you'll discover that none of them will make the time values all read the same.
5 The gray notes are important. Do these remind you of something you saw earlier in the book?
6 Look at page 5. These are different time zones.
7 Use the clocks on page 5 to work out how the different time zones relate to one another. For example, CET is one hour ahead of GMT.
8 To make the GMT and CET displays match, the CET clock needs to have a time that is 1 hour ahead of the GMT time. For example, 22:00 on the GMT clock would match 23:00 on the CET clock.
9 The PST clock needs to display a time that is 8 hours before the GMT clock.
10 The EST clock needs to display a time that is 5 hours before the GMT clock.

LUNAR PLAIN

1 There are ten different places where you can enter the lunar plain map. The best way to solve this puzzle is just to try one and see what happens. You might find it easier if you use a small object to keep track of where you are.
2 You can't enter in the first row. If you enter in the second, seventh, eighth, ninth, or tenth rows, you can't reach the other side of the map.
3 You should enter in the fourth row.
4 Most of your moves are forced. Once you enter in the fourth row, you must then move down the page after you reach the first obstacle. Then you must go right, and so on.

PAGES 16–17
KEY PANEL

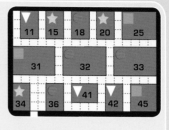

1 Each of the four lines on the clue card refers to one of the four codes, A to D.
2 The panel shows that each code has four digits.
3 On the clue card, the first and third clues refer to famous dates in space history that are given earlier in the book.
4 The second and fourth clues should be read out loud, reading each word separately. Some of the words sound like numbers!
5 What do you think Alpha, Bravo, Charlie, and Delta refer to? Are the capital letters important?
6 These words are the phonetic alphabet code words for the letter of the alphabet they start with, so, for example, "Charlie" gives the solution to code C.

PAGES 16–17
SECURITY PANEL

1 Is there a type of puzzle in which you have seen crossed-out clues before?
2 Have you ever solved a wordsearch puzzle?
3 The crossed-out numbers can be found written in different directions on the panel screen.
4 If you were to imagine solving this puzzle like a wordsearch with numbers, by crossing out all the numbers from the ID card, what would be left?
5 Try copying out the puzzle if you find it too hard to do in your head.

PAGES 18–19
LIGHTING SYSTEM

1 Start with the number at the top, 64820, then follow the arrows and apply the various operations that are described in the boxes.
2 Follow each different color of arrow, applying each operation described in turn. For example, the yellow arrows start by adding the digits in 64820, to give 20 (6+4+8+2+0), then dividing by 10, giving 2. Then it divides by 2 again, giving 1, which is the first mystery digit in the middle of the diagram.
3 When the blue arrow leaves one of the boxes in two different directions, follow each one individually.

PAGES 18–19
HANGAR MAP

1 Clue 8 tells you that the Waste Disposal room is exactly twice the size of the Cafe. This clue lets you be certain which is the Waste Disposal room since there is only one room that is exactly twice the size of another.
2 Room 25 is the size of twelve tiles, which is twice the size of the various six-tile rooms. The other room sizes are nine and fifteen tiles, neither of which are twice the size of another room. So room 25 is the Waste Disposal.
3 Clue 7 refers to the sum of three room numbers. The lowest possible sum of three numbers is 11+15+18 = 44, but there is only one room that this can be, so room 45 must be the Tool Storage, and the Silos must be rooms 11, 15, and 18, since if any other room was used instead, then the total would be greater than 45.
4 Clue 3 makes it clear that the Recreation Room must be room 20.
5 From clue 1, the Guard Room must be room 34—rooms 25 and 45 are already assigned.
6 Clue 5 tells us that the room numbers of one of the Laboratories plus the Medical Facility add up to 65 since we have already identified these rooms. This means they must be rooms 32 and 33 because there are no other pairs of rooms that add up to 65. From clue 2, we know the Laboratories aren't separated and are the same size, so the Laboratories must be rooms 31 and 32, and the Medical Facility must be room 33.
7 Clue 6 tells us that the Safe Room must be room 36.
8 Clue 4 tells us that room 41 is the Crew Supplies, and room 42 is the Cafe.

PAGES 20–21
IDENTITY CODE

1 You're looking at a reflection of your space suit in the panel, so the writing is reflected too!
2 The information you want is in the larger text behind the right-way-around writing.
3 The bottom line of information is a common name. The top line is a number.

PAGES 20–21
RETRIEVING THE FUEL

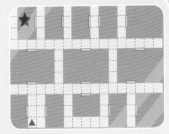

1 The up arrows represent forward moves, and the arrows that curve to the right or left represent 90 degree turns to the right or left as appropriate. The numbers before the forward moves represent the number of squares you will move. Find a series of commands that takes you to the starred room.

2 There may appear to be lots of options, but in most cases there is only one move that doesn't involve crashing into any walls!

3 All the doors are open. You may need to travel through rooms as part of your route and imagine the grid squares within them when counting.

4 The first move is command C. This takes you to the tile beneath the bottom-left corner of the center room.

5 The next command should take you through the center room and out the other side.

6 You need a total of six commands to reach the fuel, which means you will need to use at least one command more than once.

PAGES 22–23
ROUTING DIAGRAMS

1 Each diagram is a separate puzzle. For the puzzle with letters, join pairs of letters instead of numbers.

2 In the number puzzle, the path for the 6 runs around the outside edge of the grid.

PAGES 22–23
LOADING PLAN

1 Look for fuel pods that are visually different from the others and find their matching pairs first. Write out a list of letters, A to N, and cross them off as you assign them to pairs.

2 Pods E and K have more notches than the other pods, so they must form a pair.

3 Pod C has a very simple design, so it must match pod L.

PAGES 24–25
PROGRAMMING YOUR JOURNEY HOME

1 Look at the center row and column of the middle puzzle. Notice that no number repeats in any row or column. Each row and column of each puzzle must contain numbers 1 through 5.

2 There are large letters in the background of each puzzle, identifying the X, Y, and Z angles.

3 Each puzzle has a highlighted square. Find the value that goes in this square. You can do this without copying out and solving all of each puzzle, but you might prefer to copy and solve the whole puzzle anyway.

PAGES 24–25
THRUST

1 Digit 1 – this is from page 7.

2 Digit 2 – this is from page 16.

3 Digit 3 – this is from page 11. Add up the value of each of the six shapes, then divide by 4.

4 Digit 4 – count the number of doors on the map on page 21, then divide by 2. Don't count the bottom entrance door since this doesn't open into a room.

5 Digit 5 – look at the map on page 8 and count the number of houses, then divide by 4.

PAGES 24–25
BURN TIME

1 Digit 1 – this is from page 10.

2 Digit 2 – this is from page 14.

3 Digit 3 – this is from page 11.

4 Digit 4 – this is from page 18.

5 Digit 5 – this is from page 21. How many times did you use command C in the ultimate solution?

SPACE PUZZLES SOLUTIONS

PAGES 6–7
BAY DOORS
The code is

None of the other codes can be dialed.

DOCKING CLAMPS
A1, B2, C3

PAGES 8–9
LAUNCH COORDINATES
The launch site is E2.

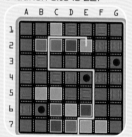

DESTINATION CODE
The letters are mirrored, like this:

A = A   D = Ⅱ   F = ꟼ
B = ⨁   E = ⨁   G = ◊
C = ◊

So the solution is:

PAGES 10–11
ODD STAR CHART
Join the odd dots in increasing order to reveal the constellation of Cassiopeia.

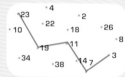

ROCKET SCIENCE

19	-13	÷3	+18	-2	**18**
12	÷2	×5	+1	-5	**26**
15	+15	-18	×5	+12	**5**
19	-7	÷3	+5	-3	**6**
5	×12	÷6	+7	×2	**34**

PAGES 12–13
MEASURING FUEL
Transfer as follows:
C to B; B to A; A to C;
B to A; A to C.

BALANCING FUEL LEVELS
The five-pointed star weighs 2 pounds, the hexagon weighs 4 pounds, the circle weighs 3 pounds, and the square weighs 6 pounds.

PAGES 14–15
DOOR LOCK MECHANISM
The times should all read the equivalent of 23:00GMT, so the correct sequence is +++/--/+/-

PAGES 14–15
LUNAR PLAIN

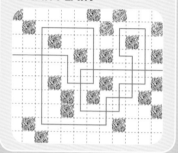

PAGES 16–17
KEY PANEL
A: 1240; B: 1969; C: 1961; D: 6842

A and D should be read out loud because some of the words sound like numbers: Won (1), too (2), for (4), nothing (0), sicks! (6), Ate (8), for (4), and two! (2). The other two refer to dates given in a picture beneath the Introduction on page 5.

SECURITY PANEL
After crossing out the numbers that appear in the grid, there is one number left in each column, so from left to right you can read off 323065, corresponding with the six empty spaces at the bottom of the panel. (If you answered 303652, reading left to right and top to bottom, the computer will accept that too).

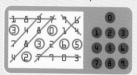

PAGES 18–19
LIGHTING SYSTEM
The solution is 6861, which can be calculated as follows:

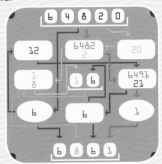

HANGAR MAP

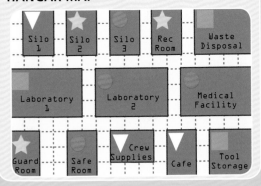

PAGES 20–21
IDENTITY CODE
The information from the space suit is mirrored in the reflection, so the ID is 8088 and the name is TIMOTHY.

RETRIEVING THE FUEL
The solution is C B C A E D, as illustrated on this map. The colors match those of the commands next to the puzzle:

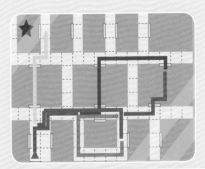

PAGES 22–23
ROUTING DIAGRAMS

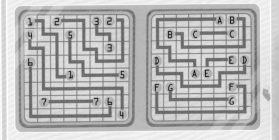

LOADING PLAN
The pairs are A-G, B-H, C-L, D-J, E-K, F-N, I-M.

PAGES 24–25
PROGRAMMING YOUR JOURNEY HOME
The X Angle is 5, the Y Angle is 1, and the Z Angle is 5.

4	1	5	3	2
5	3	2	4	1
1	4	3	2	5
3	2	1	5	4
2	5	4	1	3

4	3	1	2	5
3	5	2	1	4
1	4	5	3	2
2	1	4	5	3
5	2	3	4	1

4	5	3	1	2
3	1	4	2	5
5	3	2	4	1
1	2	5	3	4
2	4	1	5	3

THRUST
22588
BURN TIME
24972

INDEX

THE AUTHOR

Dr. Gareth Moore is the author of a wide range of puzzle and brain-training books for both children and adults, including *The Kids' Book of Puzzles*, *The Mammoth Book of Brain Games*, and *The Rough Guide Book of Brain Training*. He is also the founder of the daily brain-training website www.BrainedUp.com. He earned his PhD from Cambridge University (UK) in the field of computer speech recognition, teaching machines to understand spoken words.